READ THESE
BANNED
BOOKS

A Journal And 52-Week
Reading Challenge

from the American Library Association

ALAAmericanLibraryAssociation

sourcebooks

The reviews in this book come from *Booklist*. *Booklist* is the book review magazine of the American Library Association and a vibrant source of reading recommendations for all readers. It's been considered an essential collection development and readers' advisory tool by thousands of librarians for more than 100 years. For more information, visit booklistonline.com.

Published by Sourcebooks
P.O. Box 4410, Naperville, Illinois 60567-4410
(630) 961-3900
sourcebooks.com

Printed and bound in the United States of America.
VP 10 9 8 7 6 5 4 3 2 1

CONTENTS

INTRODUCTION

Welcome, rebel reader!

This one-year reading journey invites you to celebrate the freedom to read. Included are fifty-two books that have been challenged or banned as documented by the American Library Association.

Your goal is not just to complete each title but also to revel in unrestricted reading. Here's what you can expect: Each week you will be introduced to a new title to read and cross off your list. A short write-up and review from the ALA will whet your appetite for the work, and a paired writing prompt will inspire you to explore and record your thoughts as you read. The selected titles span categories, from fiction to fantasy to graphic novels and more, and all have, at one time or another, been targeted for removal or restriction in schools and libraries.

Banning books is a threat to freedom of speech and freedom of choice; reading banned books is an opportunity to stand up for these freedoms.

Are you ready to read?

WHY ARE THESE BOOKS BANNED?

The American Library Association's Office for Intellectual Freedom tracks challenges to library, school, and university materials and services. Here are the documented reasons why the books featured in this volume were challenged, censored, or banned.

The Absolutely True Diary of a Part-Time Indian, Sherman Alexie

Reasons: profanity, sexual references, and allegations of sexual misconduct by the author

The House of the Spirits, Isabel Allende

Reasons: sexually explicit, religious viewpoint, violence, immoral, culturally insensitive, offensive language, occult-satanism, unsuited for age group, abortion

Speak, Laurie Halse Anderson

Reasons: political viewpoint, biased against male students, inclusion of rape and profanity

***I Know Why the Caged Bird Sings*, Maya Angelou**

Reasons: offensive language, sexually explicit

***Thirteen Reasons Why*, Jay Asher**

Reasons: drugs/alcohol/smoking, sexually explicit, suicide, unsuited for age group

***The Handmaid's Tale*, Margaret Atwood**

Reasons: profanity and "vulgarity and sexual overtones"

***Fun Home: A Family Tragicomic*, Alison Bechdel**

Reasons: violence, "graphic images"

***Something Happened in Our Town: A Child's Story about Racial Injustice*, Marianne Celano, Marietta Collins, and Ann Hazzard, illustrated by Jennifer Zivoin**

Reasons: anti-police views, "divisive language"

***The Perks of Being a Wallflower*, Stephen Chbosky**

Reasons: homosexuality, offensive language, sexually explicit, unsuited to age group

***The Kingdom of Little Wounds*, Susann Cokal**

Reasons: sexually explicit, violence, "belittles women"

***The Hunger Games*, Suzanne Collins**

Reasons: sexually explicit, violence, unsuited to age group

***This Book Is Gay*, Juno Dawson, illustrated by Spike Gerrell**

Reasons: LGBTQIA+ and sexual content, "pure propaganda"

***Whale Talk*, Chris Crutcher**

Reasons: racism, offensive language

***Nickel and Dimed: On (Not) Getting By in America*, Barbara Ehrenreich**

Reasons: drugs, inaccurate, offensive language, political viewpoint, religious viewpoint

***Lawn Boy*, Jonathan Evison**

Reasons: LGBTQIA+ content, profanity, sexually explicit, promoting a political agenda

***Extremely Loud and Incredibly Close*, Jonathan Safran Foer**

Reason: sexually explicit

***Dreaming in Cuban*, Cristina García**

Reasons: political viewpoint, sexually explicit

Melissa, Alex Gino

Reasons: LGBTQIA+ content, conflicting with a religious viewpoint, and not reflecting "the values of our community"

Looking for Alaska, John Green

Reasons: offensive language, sexually explicit, and unsuited for age group

Prince & Knight, Daniel Haack, illustrated by Stevie Lewis

Reasons: LGBTQIA+ content; for being "a deliberate attempt to indoctrinate young children" with the potential to cause confusion, curiosity, and gender dysphoria; and for conflicting with a religious viewpoint

The Curious Incident of the Dog in the Night-Time, Mark Haddon

Reasons: offensive language, religious viewpoint, unsuited for age group, "profanity and atheism"

The 1619 Project: A New Origin Story, Nikole Hannah-Jones and the New York Times Magazine, edited by Caitlin Roper, Ilena Silverman, and Jake Silverstein

Reasons: political and historical viewpoint

I Am Jazz, **Jessica Herthel and Jazz Jennings, illustrated by Shelagh McNicholas**

Reasons: LGBTQIA+ content, for a transgender character, and for confronting a topic that is "sensitive, controversial, and politically charged"

Crank, **Ellen Hopkins**

Reasons: drugs, offensive language, sexually explicit

The Kite Runner, **Khaled Hosseini**

Reasons: sexual violence, religious viewpoint, and was thought to "lead to terrorism" and "promote Islam"

The Color of Earth, **Kim Dong Hwa**

Reasons: nudity, sex education, sexually explicit, unsuited to age group

All Boys Aren't Blue, **George M. Johnson**

Reasons: LGBTQIA+ content, sexually explicit

Beyond Magenta: Transgender Teens Speak Out, **Susan Kuklin**

Reasons: LGBTQIA+ content, sexually explicit, biased, and for "its effect on any young people who would read it"

***Two Boys Kissing*, David Levithan**

Reason: LGBTQIA+ content, image of two boys kissing, "condones public displays of affection"

***Fallen Angels*, Walter Dean Myers**

Reason: drugs, offensive language, racism, sexual content, violence

***The Things They Carried*, Tim O'Brien**

Reasons: profanity, sexual content, "controversial"

***Out of Darkness*, Ashley Hope Pérez**

Reasons: sexually explicit, depictions of abuse

***The Golden Compass*, Philip Pullman**

Reasons: political viewpoint, religious viewpoint, violence

***Stamped: Racism, Antiracism, and You*, Jason Reynolds and Ibram X. Kendi**

Reasons: author's public statements, "selective storytelling incidents," and does not encompass racism against all people

***All American Boys*, Jason Reynolds and Brendan Kiely**

Reasons: profanity, drug use, and alcoholism, anti-police views, divisive topics, and "too much of a sensitive matter right now"

And Tango Makes Three, **Justin Richardson and Peter Parnell, illustrated by Henry Cole**

Reasons: anti-family, homosexuality, political viewpoint, religious viewpoint, unsuited for age group, "promotes the homosexual agenda"

Eleanor & Park, **Rainbow Rowell**

Reason: offensive language

Persepolis: The Story of a Childhood, **Marjane Satrapi**

Reasons: gambling, offensive language, political viewpoint, "politically, racially, and socially offensive," "graphic depictions"

What My Mother Doesn't Know, **Sonya Sones**

Reasons: nudity, offensive language, sexually explicit

Revolutionary Voices: A Multicultural Queer Youth Anthology, **edited by Amy Sonnie**

Reasons: homosexuality, sexually explicit

Maus: A Survivor's Tale, **Art Spiegelman**

Reasons: culturally insensitive, political viewpoint, "rough, objectionable language," and a drawing of a nude woman

This One Summer, Mariko Tamaki, illustrated by Jillian Tamaki

Reasons: profanity, sexual references, and certain illustrations

Drama, Raina Telgemeier

Reasons: LGBTQIA+ content and for concerns that it goes against "family values/morals"

The Hate U Give, Angie Thomas

Reasons: profanity, anti-police messaging, drug use, and sexual references

Habibi, Craig Thompson

Reasons: nudity, sexually explicit, and unsuited for age group

A Day in the Life of Marlon Bundo, Jill Twiss, illustrated by EG Keller

Reasons: LGBTQIA+ content and political viewpoints, "designed to pollute the morals of its readers," and "for not including a content warning"

The Color Purple, Alice Walker

Reasons: homosexuality, offensive language, sexually explicit

The Glass Castle, Jeannette Walls

Reasons: offensive language, sexually explicit

So Far from the Bamboo Grove, Yoko Kawashima Watkins

Reasons: culturally insensitive, violence, a reference to rape, inaccurate portrayal of Korean/Japanese relations

Nasreen's Secret School, Jeanette Winter

Reasons: religious viewpoint, violence, unsuited to age group

The Autobiography of Malcolm X as Told to Alex Haley, Malcolm X and Alex Haley

Reasons: violence, political viewpoint, racist language

Front Desk, Kelly Yang

Reasons: political viewpoint, considered to be teaching anti-racism

READING LOG

Titles completed and everything else I am reading

DATE STARTED	TITLE	DATE COMPLETED

DATE STARTED	TITLE	DATE COMPLETED

DATE STARTED	TITLE	DATE COMPLETED

The Absolutely True Diary of a Part-Time Indian

SHERMAN ALEXIE

Arnold Spirit, a goofy-looking dork with a decent jump shot, spends his time lamenting life on the "poor-ass" Spokane Indian reservation, drawing cartoons and, along with his aptly named pal Rowdy, laughing those laughs over anything and nothing that affix best friends so intricately together. When a teacher pleads with Arnold to want more, to escape the hopelessness of the rez, Arnold switches to a rich white school and immediately becomes as much an outcast in his own community as he is a curiosity in his new one. He weathers the typical teenage indignations and triumphs like a champ but soon faces far more trying ordeals as his home life begins to crumble and decay amid the suffocating mire of alcoholism on the reservation.

Write about a time when you struggled to fit in.

The House of the Spirits

ISABEL ALLENDE

In this debut novel, author Isabel Allende, niece of Chilean President Salvador Allende who was slain in the military coup of 1973, has written a compelling family chronicle. Patriarch Esteban dreams of politics and his clairvoyant wife Clara. Their daughter, Blanca, infuriates her father by falling deeply in love with the peasant Pedro. Alba, beloved granddaughter of Esteban and daughter of Blanca and Pedro, is a revolutionary who leads the family into a hopeful future. Allende's portrait of the Trueba clan and her picture of an unnamed country's political history creates a splendid and fantastic meditation on a people and a nation victimized and brutalized by their past.

Who are the key characters in your family chronicle? How would you describe each of them?

Speak

LAURIE HALSE ANDERSON

Having broken up an end-of-summer party by calling the police, high school freshman Melinda Sordino begins the school year as a social outcast. What her fellow students do not know is that she was raped at the party by Andy Evans, a popular upperclassman, and calling the police was her attempt to get help. Unable to speak to the police or anyone else about her tragic encounter, she becomes a pariah, slipping into the solitary role of suffering from alienation and self-loathing. Slowly, with the help of an eccentric and understanding art teacher, she begins to recover from the trauma, only to find Andy threatening her again.

When have you felt powerless in your life? How did you regain your power?

I Know Why the Caged Bird Sings

MAYA ANGELOU

In this autobiographical account of the growing-up years of a Southern Black girl, author Maya Angelou describes her early years living with her indomitable grandmother, who owned the only Negro general merchandise store in Stamps, Arkansas; a stay with her mother in St. Louis that ended when the then eight-year-old Maya was raped; the resumption of life in Stamps; and her eventual return to her mother in California. The narrative ends when, at sixteen and unmarried, she gives birth to a son. Angelou evokes the harshness of Black Southern life while also recalling good times and bringing to life the people who played a role in her early years.

Write a story from your growing-up years.

Thirteen Reasons Why

JAY ASHER

When Clay Jensen plays the cassette tapes he received in a mysterious package, he's surprised to hear the voice of dead classmate Hannah Baker. He's one of thirteen people who receive Hannah's story, which details the circumstances that led to her suicide. Clay spends the rest of the day and long into the night listening to Hannah's words, which illuminate betrayals and secrets that demonstrate the consequences of even small actions. She calls out Justin, who is responsible for rumors about her; Alex, who told others that Hannah had the "best ass" in town; and Jessica and Courtney, who pretended to be her friends when they were only using her. Also mentioned is Ryan, who stole Hannah's poem "Soul Alone," and published it in the school newspaper. As he listens to Hannah name students who bullied her, Clay wonders what he could have done to help her.

Write about a time you wish you had done something differently.

_____

_____

_____

_____

The Handmaid's Tale

MARGARET ATWOOD

Offred is a Handmaid in the near-future society of Gilead. Pollution has caused an epidemic of infertility, so fertile women are forced to become Handmaids and are assigned to a Commander in order to conceive. Offred wistfully remembers her husband and daughter, and what it was like to wear clothes of her own choosing and read good books; she recalls when she had a job, money of her own, and access to knowledge. But all of that is gone. Now everyone has a role to play. And day-to-day life in Gilead, which was created to be a utopia, is tinged with threatening undertones.

What personal liberty would you miss most if it were taken away? Why?

Fun Home: A Family Tragicomic

ALISON BECHDEL

This autobiographical coming-out story is largely about father and daughter. Author Alison Bechdel's mother and two brothers are in it, of course, but her father, Bruce Bechdel, had the biggest impact on his eldest child and so is naturally the other main character in her graphic novel. After disclosing her lesbianism in a letter home from college, her mother replied that her father was homosexual too. Alison suddenly understood his legal trouble over buying a beer for a teenage boy, all the teen male "helpers" he had around the house, and his solo outings during family vacations to New York. This memoir, which uses her childhood journals as a source, captures the fraught family dynamic.

Describe a memory centered on your father.

Something Happened in Our Town: A Child's Story about Racial Injustice

MARIANNE CELANO, MARIETTA COLLINS, AND ANN HAZZARD, ILLUSTRATED BY JENNIFER ZIVOIN

In this picture book, a Black man is shot by a white cop, and Emma and Josh, classmates in Ms. Garcia's class, learn about the incident from older students. Somewhat confused by what they are hearing, they ask their parents to explain the shooting and the protests that have erupted in the streets of their town. The story follows the discussions in two different homes: with Emma's white family and Josh's Black one. Older siblings offer their views, and in the process, Emma and Josh learn about the complicated history of race relations in our nation. They also learn the roles they can play in making all their friends and classmates feel included. When Omad, a new student from another country, joins their class, Emma and Josh step up and speak out against the soccer team that wants to exclude him.

Write about a time you stood up and spoke out. What inspired you to do it?

The Perks of Being a Wallflower

STEPHEN CHBOSKY

This is the story of Charlie, a fifteen-year-old wallflower, an outsider and observer, with a passion for books, music, and soul-searching. Before the start of high school, Charlie's best (and only) friend kills himself, leaving Charlie alone and unmoored. As he slowly adapts to a new school, Charlie experiences a series of firsts: parties, experiments with drugs and alcohol, and romantic relationships. He vacillates between full involvement in the crazy course of his life and backing off completely. Eventually, he discovers that to be a whole person who knows how to be a real friend, he must confront his past— and remember what his beloved, deceased Aunt Helen did to him.

What secrets do you keep from your friends?

DATE STARTED:

DATE FINISHED:

MY RATING:

☆ ☆ ☆ ☆ ☆

The Kingdom of Little Wounds

SUSANN COKAL

Skyggehavn, a fictional sixteenth-century kingdom, is a desperate place plagued by madness, disease, and mercury poisoning. Political intrigue, murder, and manipulation abound in this troubling tale of Ava, an aspiring royal seamstress, and Midi, a mute foreign nurse-maid, who together orchestrate a daring gambit to ensure both the continued power of the reigning queen and the downfall of the cruel man who sadistically took advantage of them both. The crooked fairy tales woven throughout this dark story underscore the grim realities of the women who suffer terrible violence at the hands of brutal men, until Ava and Midi, whose indignation simmers, enact a gruesome form of revenge.

When has your indignation simmered? Did you seek revenge?

The Hunger Games

SUZANNE COLLINS

Sixteen-year-old Katniss poaches food for her widowed mother and little sister from the forest outside the legal perimeter of District 12, the poorest of the dozen districts constituting Panem, the North American dystopic state that has replaced the United States in the not-too-distant future. Her hunting and tracking skills serve her well when she is cast into the nation's annual Hunger Games, a fight to the death where contestants must battle harsh terrain, artificially concocted weather conditions, and two teenaged contestants from each of Panem's districts. District 12's second "tribute" is Peeta, the baker's son, who has been in love with Katniss since he was five. Although Katniss may be skilled with a bow and arrow and adept at analyzing her opponents' next moves, she has much to learn about personal sentiments, especially her own.

Describe the dystopic state you would most fear.

DATE STARTED:

DATE FINISHED:

MY RATING:

☆ ☆ ☆ ☆ ☆

Whale Talk

CHRIS CRUTCHER

Adopted, biracial high school senior The Tao Jones (his birth mother seems to "have been a little too 'spiritual'") is well-adjusted on the surface. A smart, likable kid with a great sense of humor and athletic ability, he glides through academia with everything an adolescent boy needs—decent grades and female companionship. What T. J. doesn't need is competitive sports, which Cutter High School jocks and coaches see as a personal snub. T. J.'s resolve weakens, however, when English teacher–coach Mr. Simet makes an unconventional offer: be the anchor of the swim team and pick your fellow fish. Perfect, especially since racist football bully Mike Barbour has taken up letter jackets as a cause. It seems developmentally disabled Chris Coughlin has been wearing his dead brother's jacket, and Mike is annoyed. If Chris, naturally comfortable in the water, is on the swim team, T. J. reasons, Chris will earn a jacket of his own, and Mike will be put in his place.

Describe a time when you stood up for a friend.

Read These Banned Books

This Book Is Gay

JUNO DAWSON, ILLUSTRATED BY SPIKE GERRELL

Often breezy in tone but always informative, Juno Dawson's book is filled with facts and stories about being lesbian, gay, bisexual, transgender, or, as the author puts it, anywhere within "the full and infinite spectrum of sexual and gender identities." Aimed at straight readers as well as gay ones, Dawson's book is witty and wise and so packed with information it's hard to imagine a reader who won't learn something new. (Did you know a gay guy with a penchant for sportswear and man jewelry is called a scallie?) Illustrated with clever cartoon art, the book is generally upbeat while honestly acknowledging downsides of being LGBTQ, such as homophobia and bullying.

Write about an LGBTQ person that you admire.

Nickel and Dimed: On (Not) Getting By in America

BARBARA EHRENREICH

How does a single mother (or anyone else) leaving welfare survive without government assistance in the form of food stamps, Medicaid, and housing and childcare subsidies? To find the answers, author and social critic Barbara Ehrenreich left her home in Key West and traveled from Florida to Maine and then to Minnesota, working in low-paying jobs. Ehrenreich, who holds a PhD in biology, resolved not to fall back on any skills derived from her education or usual work and to take the cheapest accommodations in motels and trailer parks as long as there was "an acceptable level of safety and privacy." The "working poor," Ehrenreich concludes, "are in fact the major philan-thropists of our society. They neglect their own children so that the children of others will be cared for; they live in substandard housing so that other homes will be shiny and perfect; they endure privation so that inflation will be low and stock prices high."

What was the lowest-paying job you ever held? Was it a springboard or a dead end?

Lawn Boy

JONATHAN EVISON

Meet Mike Muñoz, a twenty-two-year-old landscaper who spends his days mowing lawns and edging flower beds, his evenings taking care of his disabled brother, and his nights dreaming about elaborate topiary and writing the great American novel. When Mike is fired for refusing to pick up rain-sodden St. Bernard feces, he embarks on a path of self-discovery that introduces an eccentric cast of characters, including a shrewd entrepreneur with questionable business practices, an ambitious but unscrupulous realtor, an eccentric housemate who provides bass guitar accompaniment while watching classic porn, a group of hipster bearded baristas who favor artisanal sandwiches, and Andrew, a philosophical librarian with an activist streak. What will Mike Muñoz learn about happiness and authenticity?

Describe the cast of characters in your life.

Extremely Loud
and Incredibly Close

JONATHAN SAFRAN FOER

Oskar Schell is a nine-year-old amateur inventor and Shakespearean actor. But Oskar's boots, as he likes to say, are very heavy—his father, whom he worshipped, perished in the World Trade Center on 9/11. In his dad's closet a year later, Oskar finds a key in a vase mysteriously labeled "Black." So he goes searching after the lock it opens, visiting (alphabetically) everyone listed in the phone book with the surname Black. Oskar's journey leads him through the five boroughs of New York and into contact with survivors of all sorts. Will he find what he is looking for?

Describe a journey of discovery you've recently taken. What did you learn?

Dreaming in Cuban

CRISTINA GARCÍA

For three generations of Cuban women, the ties that bind are impassioned and profound. Matriarch Celia del Pino resides by the sea in Castro's Cuba. She is a romantic and strongly supports socialism. Daughter Felicia, who is bewitched by voodoo, suffers delusions brought on by her husband's "gift" of syphilis, while in Brooklyn, daughter Lourdes converses with her dead father. Granddaughter Pilar favors music by the Sex Pistols but yearns for the homeland and a visit with her grandmother. For the del Pino women, divided by politics and geography, there will be no agreement on Castro or the Revolution.

What are the ties that bind your family across generations? What divides you?

Melissa

ALEX GINO

Ten-year-old George has a secret. Everyone thinks she is a boy, but inside she knows that she is really a girl named Melissa. When her fourth-grade class prepares to mount a dramatic production of *Charlotte's Web*, George knows that more than anything in the world, she wants to play the part of Charlotte. But things aren't that simple. Boys don't play girls' parts, her teacher insists as she denies George the chance to audition. But not all is lost. George and her best friend, Kelly, devise a plan to save the day and let the entire class know of George's true identity. (Note: This book was previously titled *George*; the title has been changed in later editions.)

Have you ever felt excluded because of your gender? Write about your experience.

DATE STARTED:

DATE FINISHED:

MY RATING:

☆ ☆ ☆ ☆ ☆

Looking for Alaska

JOHN GREEN

Sixteen-year-old Miles Halter leaves his boring life in Florida in hopes of boarding school adventures in Alabama. A collector of famous last words, Miles is after what the dying François Rabelais called "the Great Perhaps." At the boarding school, he is blessed with a fast-talking and quick-witted roommate who just so happens to be friends with the enigmatic and beautiful Alaska Young. It's Alaska who introduces Miles to the purported last words of Simón Bolívar: "Damn it. How will I ever get out of this labyrinth?" It is a question that haunts Miles as he and his friends are forced to cope with loss.

Write your own "last words." Why did you choose them?

Prince & Knight

DANIEL HAACK, ILLUSTRATED BY STEVIE LEWIS

Once upon a time, a handsome young prince lived in a very grand kingdom. His parents, the king and queen, wish to find him a companion before he is old enough to take the throne. The three set out on a quest to find a suitable princess. While out searching, the prince hears of a dragon ravaging his kingdom and immediately rides out to fight it. At first, he faces the dragon alone, but then a knight on horseback arrives to help him. Together, they defeat the dragon. The two gaze lovingly into one another's eyes, and it is clear to the prince that the search for a partner is done. The kingdom celebrates, and so do the king and queen, on the wedding day of the prince and his knight.

Describe your happily-ever-after.

The Curious Incident of the Dog in the Night-Time

MARK HADDON

The hero of this book is fifteen-year-old Christopher Boone, an autistic math genius who has just discovered the dead body of his neighbor's poodle, Wellington. Wellington was killed with a garden fork, and Christopher decides that, like his idol Sherlock Holmes, he's going to find the killer. Wellington's owner, Mrs. Shears, refuses to speak to Christopher about the matter, and his father tells him to stop investigating. As the mystery of Wellington's death begins to unveil the answers to questions in his own life, Christopher, who is unable to grasp even the most basic emotions, struggles with the reality of a startling deception.

What mysteries, big or small, are you curious about?

The 1619 Project:
A New Origin Story

NIKOLE HANNAH-JONES AND THE *NEW YORK TIMES MAGAZINE*, EDITED BY CAITLIN ROPER, ILENA SILVERMAN, AND JAKE SILVERSTEIN

Author Nikole Hannah-Jones launched The 1619 Project in 2019 in the *New York Times Magazine* to mark the 400th anniversary of the arrival of the first captive Africans to colonial soil in Virginia, and to take fresh measure of what followed as a new nation gradually coalesced, then failed to live up to its founding ideals. The response was passionate, paving the way for this volume of expanded and new essays, each preceded by a historical photograph and a history-inspired poem or work of fiction. Long-concealed incidents and individuals, causes and effects are brought to light by Hannah-Jones and seventeen other vital thinkers and clarion writers, each of whom sharpens our understanding of the dire influence of anti-Black racism, how infra-structure enforces racial inequality, the unrelenting financial struggle in Black families and communities, and how Black Americans fighting for equality decade after decade have preserved our democracy.

Share a story about someone you know who stood up against injustice.

DATE STARTED:

DATE FINISHED:

MY RATING:

☆ ☆ ☆ ☆ ☆

I Am Jazz

**JESSICA HERTHEL AND JAZZ JENNINGS,
ILLUSTRATED BY SHELAGH MCNICHOLAS**

In this picture book, transgender Jazz Jennings tells her story. "I have a girl brain but a boy body," she explains, noting that from early childhood on she preferred the color pink and mermaid costumes to playing with "trucks or tools or superheroes." The book gives a clear explanation, even for the youngest, of how Jazz knew that she was born different. Teasing peers and "confused" teachers are mostly persuaded into acceptance, and Jazz is surrounded by smiling, supportive friends and family members. "I am happy. I am having fun. I am proud!" is a reassuring message for other trans children—and their families too.

Write ten positive "I am" statements.

DATE STARTED:

DATE FINISHED:

MY RATING:
☆ ☆ ☆ ☆ ☆

Crank

ELLEN HOPKINS

Sixteen-year-old Kristina lives in a comfortable, advantaged home with her caring mother and stepfather. She first tries the highly addictive drug crystal meth (or "crank") while visiting her long-estranged father, a crank junkie. While under the drug's influence, Kristina discovers her imagined, bolder self, Bree, who flirts outrageously and gets high without remorse, and when Kristina returns to her mother and family in Reno, it's Bree who makes connections with edgy guys and other crank users. What begins as a fun adventure quickly spirals out of control and into a fight for her life.

Name your bolder alter ego. Why did you pick that name?

DATE STARTED:

DATE FINISHED:

MY RATING:
☆ ☆ ☆ ☆ ☆

The Kite Runner

KHALED HOSSEINI

This story opens in Kabul in the mid-1970s. Amir is the son of a wealthy man, but his best friend is Hassan, the son of one of his father's servants. His father encourages the friendship and dotes on Hassan, who worships the ground Amir walks on. But Amir is envious of Hassan and his own father's apparent affection for the boy. One day, when Amir comes across a group of local bullies raping Hassan, he does nothing. Shamed by his own inaction, Amir pushes Hassan away, even going so far as to accuse him of stealing. Eventually, Hassan and his father are forced to leave. Years later, Amir, now living in America, receives a visit from an old family friend who gives him an opportunity to make amends for his treatment of Hassan.

Write about a time you made amends.

The Color of Earth

KIM DONG HWA

The first in a trilogy, this beautifully scripted and drawn Korean manhwa captures the intimate journey of a young girl and her widowed mother. Spanning Ehwa's life from age seven to sixteen, each chapter shows the progress of her sexual awakening. As Ehwa moves from the open curiosity of childhood that fixates on body parts to the mysteries of attraction and her own heartbreak, she and her mother navigate common issues that range from defending one's feelings from bullies (little boys in Ehwa's life; gossipy men in her mother's) to mutual attraction (a young monk and a visiting boy for Ehwa; an itinerant painter/scholar for her mother). Gradually, Ehwa begins to open her life up to love.

What is the most exhilarating experience of your life?

Read These Banned Books

All Boys Aren't Blue

GEORGE M. JOHNSON

Prominent journalist and LGBTQIA+ activist George Johnson offers his memoir-manifesto of growing up queer before he had the language to know exactly what that meant. Split into three parts, Johnson's book shares intimate stories of his childhood, adolescence, and young adulthood as he navigates family, friends, and the performance of masculinity. The personal stories—from getting his teeth kicked in as a child, to the bullying he experienced in middle school, to the isolation he suffered at his predominantly white high school—and the healing and reconciliation of self in this title are all undeniably honest and relatable—a reminder of our shared imperfection and humanity.

Write the outline to your memoir-manifesto.

DATE STARTED:

DATE FINISHED:

MY RATING:

☆ ☆ ☆ ☆ ☆

Beyond Magenta:
Transgender Teens Speak Out

SUSAN KUKLIN

Author Susan Kuklin's book profiles six transgender teens in their own words alongside the author's photographs. The result is an in-depth examination of the complexities of being transgender. The profiles are evenly divided between FTM (female to male) and MTF (male to female) teens. Also represented are a variety of races and ethnicities, one teen who is intersex, and another who regards themself as pansexual. Though their experiences differ, the teens often stress that, as the author puts it, "Gender is one variable in a person's identity, and sexual orientation is another variable. The two are not connected." This book gives faces—literally and metaphorically—to a segment of the teen population that has too long been invisible.

Find an old photo of yourself. Compare who you are right now with who you were back then.

Two Boys Kissing

DAVID LEVITHAN

Ex-boyfriends Craig and Harry are trying to set the world record for longest kiss (thirty-two hours) with a staged event in front of the high school. The story is narrated from the beyond by the "shadow uncles"—gay men of the AIDS generation—who tell millennial gay boys, "We don't want our legacy to be gravitas." These narrators marvel and remark upon Harry and Craig's kiss (a protest of hate crimes committed against a friend), the impact on two other couples at different stages of their relationships, and a hopeless loner in clear emotional danger. That "all people are born equal no matter who they kiss" sums up the message of this affecting story.

What issue would you like to protest? What form would that protest take?

Fallen Angels

WALTER DEAN MYERS

Seventeen-year-old Richie Perry is intelligent and ambitious yet faced with limited opportunity. His dilemma: what to do after high school with no money for college. It is 1967, and the Vietnam War is well underway. He enlists with the hope of using the time to get his life together and figure things out. He does not really understand what awaits him overseas—a war that will rip away his youth and test his sanity, while it forges bonds of friendship and love unlike any he has ever known. Once in Vietnam, Richie spends his time swatting bugs, tramping through rice paddies, sometimes waist deep, and fighting back the growing terror that becomes more ingrained with each patrol. In a letter home he writes, "We're all dead over here. We're all dead and just hoping we come back to life."

Write a letter to a real or fictional friend and reveal your greatest fear.

The Things They Carried

TIM O'BRIEN

"In the end...a true war story is never about war. It's about sunlight. It's about the special way that dawn spreads out on a river when you know you must cross the river and march into the mountains and do things you are afraid to. It's about love and memory. It's about sorrow. It's about sisters who never write back and people who never listen." In Tim O'Brien's world, a war story is all that—and more. This collection of twenty-two related stories has the cumulative effect of a unified novel. The "things they carry"—literally—are prosaic things: amphetamines, M16s, grenades, good-luck charms, Sterno cans, toilet paper, photographs, C rations. But the men in O'Brien's platoon—Curt Lemon, Rat Kiley, Henry Dobbins, Kiowa, and the rest—also carry less tangible but more palpable things such as disease, confusion, hatred, love, regret, fear, and what passes for courage.

What imperceptible "things" do you carry?

Out of Darkness

ASHLEY HOPE PÉREZ

Set in New London, Texas, this story revolves around the events leading up to the real-life 1937 school explosion that killed close to three hundred people. Fifteen-year-old Naomi and her younger twin siblings, Beto and Cari, have recently immigrated from Mexico to San Antonio. The biracial siblings have misgivings about the move, heightened by the presence of signs in many windows reading, "No Negroes, No Mexicans, No Dogs." Things start to look brighter when Naomi meets and then falls in love with an African American boy, Walsh, who is both brilliant and kind to her younger brother and sister, but the match is scorned by the town, and Naomi and Walsh face a dark and devastating turn of events.

How has a historical event impacted your life?

The Golden Compass

PHILIP PULLMAN

This story is set in an alternate universe much like our own but different in many ways—a world in which humans are paired with animal "daemons" that seem like alter egos, only with personalities of their own. Young Lyra Belacqua and her daemon, Pantalaimon, are being reared and educated by the Scholars at Jordon College in Oxford. Although a lackluster student, Lyra possesses an inordinate curiosity and sense of adventure. Lyra ultimately finds herself placed in the charge of the mysterious Mrs. Coulter and in possession of a rare compass-like device that can answer questions if she learns how to read it. Filled with children-stealing Gobblers, formidable armored bears, a secret scientific facility where children are being severed from their daemons, warring factions, and witch clans, it becomes evident that the future of this world and its inhabitants is in the hands of the ever-more-resilient and dedicated Lyra.

Describe your alter ego. What kind of animal daemon would it be?

Stamped: Racism, Antiracism, and You

JASON REYNOLDS AND IBRAM X. KENDI

"This is not a history book," declares author Jason Reynolds at the outset of this adaptation of Ibram X. Kendi's award-winning title, *Stamped from the Beginning*. Reynolds's "remix" begins in 1415 and travels into the present following the general outline of Kendi's comprehensive title. Through figures like Cotton Mather, W. E. B. Du Bois, and Angela Davis, among others, the thought patterns of segregationists, assimilationists, and antiracists are elucidated, along with the impact such ideas have on all aspects of American life. Throughout the book, Reynolds inserts pauses ("Record scratch") and interjects with commentary ("Let that sink in") and clarifications, making the pages not merely text, but a conversation.

What writers, thinkers, and activists have inspired you?

All American Boys

JASON REYNOLDS AND BRENDAN KIELY

Two teenage boys, one Black (Rashad) and one white (Quinn), are inextricably linked when Quinn witnesses Rashad being savagely beaten with little or no provocation by a policeman who has served as Quinn's de facto big brother since his father was killed in Afghanistan—and whose younger brother is one of Quinn's best friends. Can Quinn simply walk away from this apparent atrocity and pretend he hasn't seen what he has seen? And what of Rashad? Hospitalized with internal bleeding, all he wants is to be left alone so he can focus on his art. The challenge for both boys becomes more intense when the case becomes a cause célèbre dividing first their school and then the entire community.

Write about an issue dividing your community.

And Tango Makes Three

JUSTIN RICHARDSON AND PETER PARNELL,
ILLUSTRATED BY HENRY COLE

Roy and Silo were "a little bit different" from the other male penguins at the New York City Central Park Zoo: instead of noticing females, they noticed each other. One day, Mr. Gramzay, their keeper, watched the pining, bewildered pair make a nest together and attempt to hatch a rock. He gave them an abandoned egg instead, which they nurtured with care, and that's how Tango came to be "the only penguin in the Central Park Zoo with two daddies." This winning picture book captures the true story of two patient, loving fathers who "knew just what to do."

Write a story about your family set in a zoo.

Eleanor & Park

RAINBOW ROWELL

After a less-than-auspicious start, Eleanor and Park quietly build a relationship while riding the bus to school every day, wordlessly sharing comics and eventually music on the commute. Their worlds couldn't be more different. Park's family is idyllic: his Vietnam vet father and Korean immigrant mother are genuinely loving. Meanwhile, Eleanor and her younger siblings live in poverty under the constant threat of Richie, their abusive and controlling stepfather, while their mother inexplicably caters to his whims. Eleanor and Park's personal battles are also dark mirror images. Park struggles with the realities of falling for the school outcast, and he clashes with his father over the definition of manhood. Eleanor's fight is much more external, learning to trust her feelings about Park and navigating the sexual threat in Richie's watchful gaze.

Write a playlist to share with a friend.

DATE STARTED:

DATE FINISHED:

MY RATING:

☆ ☆ ☆ ☆ ☆

Persepolis: The Story of a Childhood

MARJANE SATRAPI

Author Marjane Satrapi's great-grandfather was Iran's last emperor, and her extraordinary autobiography in comics, which reflects her perspective from ages ten to fourteen, probably understates the violence that swirled around her during Ayatollah Khomeini's authoritarian regime. While at first her leftist parents had been for the revolution and against the Shah's regime, once the Shah departed and his government was replaced with an Islamic republic under the rule of Ayatollah Khomeini, religious extremism took hold, and the family began to fear for their lives. When war broke out between Iran and Iraq and a missile destroyed their Jewish neighbors, her parents determined to use their upper-middle-class means to get out.

Share a fiery strong opinion on something you wish was different.

What My Mother Doesn't Know

SONYA SONES

This story is about the joy and surprise of falling in love. Sophie, fourteen, thinks she has a crush on handsome Dylan, but she discovers that her most passionate feelings are for someone totally unexpected, a boy who makes her laugh and shows her how to look at the world. And when they kiss, every cell in her body is on fire. Meanwhile, she fights with her mom, who fights with Sophie's dad, and she refuses to wear a pink flowered dress to the school dance, changing into a slinky black outfit instead. Will she reveal her secret relationship to her friends?

Who do you secretly admire? Describe them.

Revolutionary Voices: A Multicultural Queer Youth Anthology

EDITED BY AMY SONNIE

"This is for the idea that I am only a sexual being... This is for the idea that queerness only has to do with sex." Jason Roe's prose poem opens this anthology with words that get in your face and under your skin. Not all the young writers featured here may be revolutionaries, but they all embrace a queer youth culture that is about gender, race, and class as much as it is about sexuality. The voices are raw and sometimes unpolished, and the language is passionate, powerful, and only occasionally graphic. What holds these selections together is the writers' urgent need to define themselves in their own terms.

What do you wish more people knew or understood about you?

Maus: A Survivor's Tale

ART SPIEGELMAN

Author Art Spiegelman takes his own life for subject matter in this stunning addition to Holocaust literature. In *Maus,* he queries his cantankerous father about what it was like to live through the Nazi occupation of Poland and the death camps. This decidedly unfrivolous comic book is first the father's story, and second, the portrayal of the son's edgy relationship with the old man. In physical decline—Vladek Spiegelman has a harrowing heart seizure during one of their conversations—he seems permanently shocked by his experiences into a personal psychology of hardship. He can give nothing but his story. His son writes and draws it forcefully. He uses a simple iconographic device to evoke the terror of his father's times: the Jews all have mice's heads; the Germans, those of cats.

Draw an icon of what you fear most.

Maus: A Survivor's Tale

This One Summer

MARIKO TAMAKI, ILLUSTRATED BY JILLIAN TAMAKI

Rose and her parents spend every summer at their lakeside cabin in Awago, right down the path from Rose's best friend, Windy, and her family. They spend lazy days collecting rocks on the beach, riding bikes, swimming, and having barbecues. But this summer, Rose's parents are constantly fighting, and her mother seems resentful and sad. Picking up on her parents' discord but unable to speak to anyone about it, Rose starts lashing out at Windy and grasping at what she thinks of as adulthood—turning up her nose at silliness (at which Windy excels), watching gory horror movies, reading fashion magazines, and joining in the bullying of a local teenage girl who finds herself in a tough spot. Will Rose and Windy's friendship endure?

Describe a childhood moment that changed how you felt about someone or something.

Drama

RAINA TELGEMEIER, ILLUSTRATED BY THE AUTHOR

Seventh grader Callie loves the theater, even if she can't sing well enough to perform in her beloved musicals. So, when her middle school launches a production of *Moon Over Mississippi*, she takes on the role of set designer instead. When drama and romance—both onstage and off—cause problems for the production, Callie finds that set design may be the easiest part of putting on a play. Callie is likable, hardworking, and enthusiastic, but she is confused about relationships and love, and she flits from crush to crush on a roller-coaster ride of emotions in this beautifully illustrated graphic novel.

Outline a musical based on your life.

The Hate U Give

ANGIE THOMAS

Sixteen-year-old Starr lives in two very different worlds: one is her home in a poor Black urban neighborhood, the other is the tony suburban prep school she attends and the white boy she dates there. Her bifurcated life changes dramatically when she is the only witness to the unprovoked police shooting of her unarmed friend Khalil and is challenged to speak out—though with trepidation—about the injustices being done in the event's wake. As the case becomes national news, violence erupts in her neighborhood, and Starr finds herself and her family caught in the middle. Difficulties are exacerbated by their encounters with the local drug lord for whom Khalil was dealing to earn money for his impoverished family. If there is to be hope for change, Starr comes to realize, it must be through the exercise of her voice, even if it puts her and her family in harm's way.

How can you use your voice to promote social justice?

DATE STARTED:

DATE FINISHED:

MY RATING:

☆ ☆ ☆ ☆ ☆

Habibi

CRAIG THOMPSON, ILLUSTRATED BY THE AUTHOR

At root, this black-and-white graphic novel is a love story about two have-nots in a desert society: Dodola, a young woman whose only currency is her body, and Zam, a slave boy she rescues and tries to shelter. Passages from the Qur'an provide reflection on Dodola's and Zam's lives as they connect, break apart, and find each other again. The fictional state of Wanatolia, where you can travel in time thousands of years simply by stepping from the midden slums to the sultan's palaces to the rapid encroachment of high-rise development, provides a polarizing backdrop of social conflict for the two as they struggle to find their way in the world.

If you could travel through time, where would you go?

A Day in the Life of Marlon Bundo

JILL TWISS, ILLUSTRATED BY EG KELLER

In this political satire, Marlon Bundo is a white rabbit that lives in a big boring house at the Naval Observatory with the Vice President. Marlon feels very alone and struggles to find ways to occupy himself. One day he goes for a hop in the garden and spots a "bunny-beautiful" male bunny. Marlon and Wesley hop through the garden, into the house, and through "Very Boring Meetings" with "Very Boring People." Marlon realizes that he isn't lonely anymore, and he says to Wesley, "I don't want to hop without you ever again." When the two announce their marriage plans, The Stink Bug, who holds the position of President, states emphatically that he is in charge and won't allow boy bunnies to marry boy bunnies. The other animals in the story don't like the attitude of The Stink Bug, and they vote him out. Marlon and Wesley have a very nice wedding ceremony performed by a female cat, with her wife as her date, and two "grooms-otters" standing by their side. Before they leave on their "Bunnymoon," the two watch Wolf Blitzer on BNN.

Pen a parody of an actual event in your life.

DATE STARTED:

DATE FINISHED:

MY RATING:

☆ ☆ ☆ ☆ ☆

The Color Purple

ALICE WALKER

Sisters Nettie and Celie are separated from one another as young girls, Celie to become the child bride and wife to a widower, and Nettie to be taken by a Black family to Africa as a missionary. Celie's marriage is a harsh and poverty-stricken arrangement, and she is sustained only by a series of trusting letters she addresses to God and to her sister. But eventually, this unhappy marriage proves to be a blessing, as it introduces Celie to a woman with whom she can find love and security. When Nettie returns after a thirty-year absence, the sisters' bond is once more made whole.

Write a short love letter to a person or place that makes you happy.

The Glass Castle

JEANNETTE WALLS

Author Jeannette Walls, who spent years trying to hide her childhood experiences, allows the story to spill out in this recollection of growing up. From her current perspective as a contributor to MSNBC online, she remembers the poverty, hunger, jokes, and bullying she and her siblings endured, and she looks back at her parents: her flighty, self-indulgent mother, a Pollyanna unwilling to assume the responsibilities of parenting; and her father, troubled, brilliant Rex, whose ability to turn his family's downward-spiraling circumstances into adventures allowed his children to excuse his imperfections until they grew old enough to understand what he had done to them—and to himself. His grand plans to build a home for the family never evolved: the hole for the foundation of the "The Glass Castle," as the dream house was called, became the family garbage dump and, of course, a metaphor for Rex Walls's life. Shocking, sad, and occasionally bitter, Walls speaks candidly, yet with surprising affection, about parents and about the strength of family ties—for both good and ill.

Write the opening paragraph to your autobiography.

Read These Banned Books

DATE STARTED:

DATE FINISHED:

MY RATING:

☆ ☆ ☆ ☆ ☆

So Far from the Bamboo Grove

YOKO KAWASHIMA WATKINS

Defeat by the Allies in 1945 brought confusion to Korea as well as to Japan. Among those cruelly affected was eleven-year-old Yoko Kawashima, who lived with her Japanese family in northern Korea. Sparing little in the way of detail, Yoko looks back on her brutalizing eight-month ordeal: separation from father and brother, Hideyo, and a frantic flight southward with her mother and older sister; a horrifying trip aboard a hospital train; her wounding and subsequent illness; scavenging garbage cans for food; cruel treatment at the hands of her classmates (they shunned her and called her names) after the women finally reached Japan; her beloved mother's death; and finally a reunion with Hideyo. This is a perspective of World War II rarely seen, and it is a vivid chronicle of a girl's maturation from whiny, pampered "pet" to responsible, self-reliant youth.

What hardship or adversity has helped you to grow?

Nasreen's Secret School

JEANETTE WINTER, ILLUSTRATED BY THE AUTHOR

In the Afghan city of Herat, little Nasreen's father is abducted by Taliban soldiers. After her mother sets out in search of him, heartbroken Nasreen lives with her grandmother, who laments that her granddaughter is forbidden to learn. Then the grandmother discovers a secret school for girls run by neighborhood women and enrolls Nasreen. Gradually, the young girl begins to heal in the outlawed classroom. In this powerful story based on true events, the grandmother's wrenching mix of sorrow and defiant hope is clear: "I still wait for my son and his wife. But the soldiers can never close the windows that have opened for my granddaughter."

What's the most courageous thing you've ever done?

Read These Banned Books

The Autobiography of Malcolm X as Told to Alex Haley

MALCOLM X AND ALEX HALEY

Malcolm X, an influential and controversial Black Muslim figure, relates his transformation from street hustler to religious and national leader in this first-person account. Born Malcolm Little, he moved to Michigan at age six after his father was killed by white supremacists. He spent years in foster homes, then as a drug dealer and pimp in New York and Boston. While in prison, he converted and joined the Nation of Islam, changed his name, and quickly became a leader in the organization. He later left the Nation of Islam but continued as an activist. Malcolm X was assassinated in February 1965, and this book—a collaboration between Malcolm and journalist Alex Haley—was published later that year.

Describe a cause you believe in.

Front Desk

KELLY YANG

When Mia Tang's parents find a new job managing the Calivista motel in Anaheim, California, it seems like the answer to their prayers: free housing and a stable, secure job, neither of which have come easy to the recent Chinese immigrants. Fifth grader Mia takes pride in working the front desk and becomes fast friends with the weeklies, for whom the motel is a semipermanent residence. But the motel's owner, Mr. Yao, is beyond mean—he's flat-out racist—so Mia enters a writing contest to win the family their very own motel. While working toward her dreams, will Mia be able to hold on to her job and help the immigrants and guests too?

Write about your dreams for the future.

APPENDIX

100 MOST BANNED AND CHALLENGED BOOKS: 2010–2019

The American Library Association's Office for Intellectual Freedom (OIF) has been documenting attempts to ban books in libraries and schools since 1990. OIF compiled this list of the most banned and challenged books from 2010–2019 by reviewing both the public and confidential censorship reports it received.

This list draws attention to literary censorship but only provides a snapshot of book challenges. About 82–97% of challenges remain unreported, estimates OIF, which compared results from several independent studies of third-party Freedom of Information Act (FOIA) requests documenting school and library book censorship with the information in its database.

OIF offers direct support to communities to defend their right to access information. If you're able, please consider a donation to OIF to ensure this important work continues.

1. *The Absolutely True Diary of a Part-Time Indian* by Sherman Alexie
2. Captain Underpants (series) by Dav Pilkey
3. *Thirteen Reasons Why* by Jay Asher

4. *Looking for Alaska* by John Green

5. *Melissa* (previously published as *George*) by Alex Gino

6. *And Tango Makes Three* by Justin Richardson and Peter Parnell

7. *Drama* by Raina Telgemeier

8. *Fifty Shades of Grey* by E. L. James

9. Internet Girls (series) by Lauren Myracle

10. *The Bluest Eye* by Toni Morrison

11. *The Kite Runner* by Khaled Hosseini

12. *The Hunger Games* by Suzanne Collins

13. *I Am Jazz* by Jessica Herthel and Jazz Jennings

14. *The Perks of Being a Wallflower* by Stephen Chbosky

15. *To Kill a Mockingbird* by Harper Lee

16. Bone (series) by Jeff Smith

17. *The Glass Castle* by Jeannette Walls

18. *Two Boys Kissing* by David Levithan

19. *A Day in the Life of Marlon Bundo* by Jill Twiss

20. *Sex is a Funny Word* by Cory Silverberg

21. Alice (series) by Phyllis Reynolds Naylor

22. *It's Perfectly Normal* by Robie H. Harris

23. *Nineteen Minutes* by Jodi Picoult

24. Scary Stories (series) by Alvin Schwartz

25. *Speak* by Laurie Halse Anderson

26. *Brave New World* by Aldous Huxley

27. *Beyond Magenta: Transgender Teens Speak Out* by Susan Kuklin

28. *Of Mice and Men* by John Steinbeck

29. *The Handmaid's Tale* by Margaret Atwood

30. *The Hate U Give* by Angie Thomas

31. *Fun Home: A Family Tragicomic* by Alison Bechdel

32. *It's a Book* by Lane Smith

33. *The Adventures of Huckleberry Finn* by Mark Twain

34. *The Things They Carried* by Tim O'Brien

35. *What My Mother Doesn't Know* by Sonya Sones

36. *A Child Called "It"* by Dave Pelzer

37. Bad Kitty (series) by Nick Bruel

38. *Crank* by Ellen Hopkins

39. *Nickel and Dimed: On (Not) Getting by in America* by Barbara Ehrenreich

40. *Persepolis: The Story of a Childhood* by Marjane Satrapi

41. *The Adventures of Super Diaper Baby* by Dav Pilkey

42. *This Day in June* by Gayle E. Pitman

43. *This One Summer* by Mariko Tamaki

44. *A Bad Boy Can Be Good for a Girl* by Tanya Lee Stone

45. *Beloved* by Toni Morrison

46. Goosebumps (series) by R. L. Stine

47. *In Our Mothers' House* by Patricia Polacco

48. *Lush* by Natasha Friend

49. *The Catcher in the Rye* by J. D. Salinger

50. *The Color Purple* by Alice Walker

51. *The Curious Incident of the Dog in the Night-Time* by Mark Haddon

52. *The Holy Bible*

53. *This Book Is Gay* by Juno Dawson

54. *Eleanor & Park* by Rainbow Rowell

55. *Extremely Loud and Incredibly Close* by Jonathan Safran Foer

56. Gossip Girl (series) by Cecily von Ziegesar

57. House of Night (series) by P. C. Cast

58. *My Mom's Having a Baby!: A Kid's Month-by-Month Guide to Pregnancy* by Dori Hillestad Butler

59. *Neonomicon* by Alan Moore

60. *The Dirty Cowboy* by Amy Timberlake

61. *The Giver* by Lois Lowry

62. *Anne Frank: The Diary of a Young Girl* by Anne Frank

63. *Bless Me, Ultima* by Rudolfo Anaya

64. *Draw Me a Star* by Eric Carle

65. *Dreaming in Cuban* by Cristina García

66. *Fade* by Lisa McMann

67. *The Family Book* by Todd Parr

68. *Feed* by M. T. Anderson

69. *Go the Fuck to Sleep* by Adam Mansbach

70. *Habibi* by Craig Thompson

71. *The House of the Spirits* by Isabel Allende

72. *Jacob's New Dress* by Sarah and Ian Hoffman

73. *Lolita* by Vladimir Nabokov

74. *Monster* by Walter Dean Myers

75. *Nasreen's Secret School* by Jeanette Winter

76. *Saga* by Brian K. Vaughan

77. *Stuck in the Middle* by Ariel Schrag

78. *The Kingdom of Little Wounds* by Susann Cokal

79. *1984* by George Orwell

80. *A Clockwork Orange* by Anthony Burgess

81. *Almost Perfect* by Brian Katcher

82. *The Awakening* by Kate Chopin

83. *Burned* by Ellen Hopkins

84. *Ender's Game* by Orson Scott Card

85. *Fallen Angels* by Walter Dean Myers

86. *Glass* by Ellen Hopkins

87. *Heather Has Two Mommies* by Lesléa Newman

88. *I Know Why the Caged Bird Sings* by Maya Angelou

89. *Madeline and the Gypsies* by Ludwig Bemelmans

90. *My Princess Boy* by Cheryl Kilodavis

91. *Prince & Knight* by Daniel Haack

92. *Revolutionary Voices: A Multicultural Queer Youth Anthology* by Amy Sonnie

93. *Skippyjon Jones* (series) by Judy Schachner

94. *So Far from the Bamboo Grove* by Yoko Kawashima Watkins

95. *The Color Trilogy* (series) by Kim Dong Hwa

96. *The Librarian of Basra* by Jeanette Winter

97. *The Walking Dead* (series) by Robert Kirkman

98. *Tricks* by Ellen Hopkins

99. *Uncle Bobby's Wedding* by Sarah S. Brannen

100. *Year of Wonders by Geraldine Brooks*

ABOUT THE AMERICAN LIBRARY ASSOCIATION

———

The American Library Association (ALA) is the foremost national organization providing resources to inspire library and information professionals to transform their communities through essential programs and services. ALA condemns censorship and works to ensure free access to information. Every year, ALA's Office for Intellectual Freedom (OIF) compiles a list of the Top 10 Most Challenged Books to inform the public about censorship in libraries and schools. The lists are based on information from media stories and voluntary reports sent to OIF from communities across the United States. In addition, OIF hosts Banned Books Week, an annual event typically held the last week of September that highlights the benefits of free and open access to information and draws attention to censorship attempts.

Learn more about how you can support the freedom to read and stay connected to what's going on in libraries at ilovelibraries.org.